Woof!

Louis Weber, CEO
Publications International, Ltd.
7373 North Cicero Avenue
Lincolnwood, Illinois 60712

www.pilbooks.com

Manufactured in China.

8 7 6 5 4 3 2 1

ISBN-13: 978-1-4127-4644-1
ISBN-10: 1-4127-4644-2

If Puppies Could Talk

Talk

The Words Behind the Wiggles

Written by Dana Bottenfield

new seasons®

Where did you come from, intriguing object?

Don't worry, I'll keep an eye on you.

Every dog must have his day.

— Jonathan Swift

Is that a box of tissues left unattended?

JACKPOT!

Animals are such agreeable friends—

they ask no questions.

They pass no criticisms.

—George Eliot

You look familiar.

There'd better be a prize at
the bottom of all this!

Bow. Wow.

I'll just bury the car keys right here to keep them safe.

Smiles are the language of love.

— J. C. and A. W. Hare

Mmmm! Yes!

A vintage classic — circa 1974.

I detect a hint of wet wool

with overtones of argyle.

I can't possibly go
anywhere in this outfit.

Could be food...could be not food.

What?

What part of "carnivore" don't you understand?

One more step and these pants are mine!

Sleep in peace and wake in joy.

—Sir Walter Scott

Triple threat!

Really? A sweater?

It's 100 degrees outside, lady.

You should see the other guy.

Puppies never take things too seriously—they just get up, move on, and start chewing on something new.

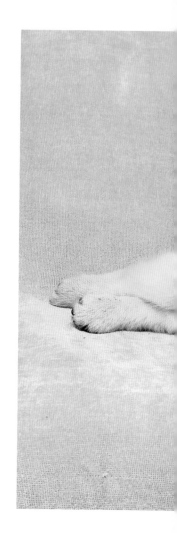

Do I smell ham?

When was there ham?

I've never found a puppy I didn't like.

Hold up,
this **so** isn't my toy...
or is it?

Nope. Not a dog.

If I stand still and think only happy thoughts,
this bath will be over in no time:
toilet water, squeaky toys, table scraps...

If I hear "double trouble" one more time,
I'm going to lose it.

I hereby claim this pot to be my hiding place for most of your stuff.

Why does this thing keep smiling at me?

Watch a puppy play in the grass and remember the simple joys life can bring.

Why would I know who knocked
the trash can over and dragged
it through the house?

Man, did I fall asleep in the wrong place...

This cardboard box

just isn't my scene.

You do not own a dog, the dog owns you.

—Unknown

Psst...

The humans are watching.

Go inside?

I think not.

Maybe if I chew this up
enough they'll get rid of it.